Better Business Writing

Capture your reader.
Make your point.
Get Results.

Copyright

Copyright 2020 by Claudia Coplon Clements

All rights reserved. No part of this book may be used or reproduced in any manner whatsoever without written permission from Claudia Coplon Clements, except in the case of brief quotations embodied in reviews.

Table of Contents

INTRODUCTION 1
So, Writing Really Is That Important? 1
What Is Relationship-Driven Writing? 2
The Material Ahead 3
How Quickly Can You Master This New Approach? 3
Will You Write Faster? 4

HURDLES AND HICCUPS 6

INFORMATION DELUGE 8

BUILDING A FOUNDATION 16
What Else Do You Avoid? 20
So What Can You Use? 23

THE WRITING PROCESS 42

EXTERNAL COMMUNICATIONS 58

STYLE AND TONE 71

INTERNAL COMMUNICATIONS 74
Emails 75
Don't Press Send Yet! 86
Informational Email Examples 87
Persuasive/Motivational Email Examples 94

NEXT STEPS 99

REFERENCE MATERIALS 101
Your Turn 102
Identifying Passive Voice 103

INTRODUCTION

Interested in improving your business writing skills? Smart.

- Good writing helps you get a job. According to the National Association of Colleges and Employers, 73.4 percent of employers want a candidate with strong written communication skills.

- Good writing helps you keep a job. Those with good writing skills are seen as more reliable, more competent and more capable.

- Good writing allows you to do your job better and leads to more opportunities. People who write well can better sell their and their organization's brand/message/service/products.

So, Writing Really Is That Important?

Almost 90 percent of what happens in today's competitive workplace is communications based. Every piece of paper or email you prepare, every report you compile adds to the information deluge your reader is experiencing. And there you are battling through that deluge to get your reader's attention, then hold his attention long enough to make your point.

Capturing and keeping today's reader demands writing skills not typically taught. Most of us have taken the long form writing we learned in school, sped it up to meet the demands of our workload, and cobbled together an approach to survive in the business world.

Sometimes it works. Usually it doesn't. How often do you find yourself placing follow-up explanatory phone calls and/or generating more information just to get your original message across? This leaves no time for thought or any kind of call to action.

It's why, when you ask many executives what they dislike most about their jobs, writing rises to the top of the list. Their dislike of writing is compounded by distracting work environments and the potential political impact of what was (or what the reader perceived to be) written. That's without including fear of the blank page or even writing itself, and the amount of time it takes to write well.

The following pages provide tools to take your writing habits apart and put them back together in a way that better attracts readers and sells your message. The philosophy behind the approach is relationship-driven writing – a proven-effective technique for structuring your written materials to better inform, persuade and/or motivate your audience.

What Is Relationship-Driven Writing?

- In long hand, relationship-driven writing is rethinking your path to putting words on paper/screen. With new thought processes, you begin writing to the reader and his needs to accomplish your goals.

- In short hand, relationship-driven writing is generating concise, decluttered material that better sells your message and your brand.

Have you been chastised for being too direct or too terse? Ignore the "being concise" goal. Tune in instead to the importance of creating a relationship with your reader. Your all too short communications are cutting your reader off at the knees and pushing her away.

The Material Ahead

As a freelance public relations writer for 30+ years, I evolved a writing approach that effectively marketed my clients. As a business writing trainer for 20+ years, I shared the lessons learned through my P.R. experience – and watched my clients decrease workloads and improve their business performance simply by making changes in the way they wrote.

Consequently, this resource is not a list of rules cast in concrete (save a few grammar hints sprinkled throughout). Rather it's a new alternative, an alternative with a track record for generating more effective materials.

The content that follows includes:

- A foundation for relationship-driven writing.

- How to approach the writing process.

- Direction on external and internal communications.

- Email etiquette tips and tricks.

How Quickly Can You Master This New Approach?

Sigh. Better writing habits cannot be formed overnight. Your best strategy is to:

- See what resonates as you read.

- Select one or two of those new writing behaviors to try.

- Put them to work over the next three weeks. It takes three weeks to break an old habit and create a new one.

- Go back for more refinements in how you write as you master each change.

Be patient. You've spent a lifetime perfecting your current habits. Breaking those habits is going to require significant effort to develop, much less make relationship-driven writing second nature.

A word to the wise: With every 'ah ha' moment, you are going to become increasingly critical of the writing coming across your desk. Resist the urge to point out their errors to others. Strangely enough, people are just never appreciative of your comments.

Will You Write Faster?

No. In fact, for the next three weeks (remember that's how long it takes to create a new habit) and for every three-week increment after you make an improvement, it is going to take longer to write. Longer, because you are thinking differently and approaching your writing from the reader's perspective.

The trade off comes in the time you <u>don't</u> have to spend with follow-up phone calls and even more written documents, emails, letters, etc. Bottom line, it's worth the investment on the front end.

If you push through that feeling of being scared, that feeling of taking risk, really amazing things can happen.
— *Marissa Mayer, CEO, Yahoo! Inc.*

Better Business Writing

HURDLES AND HICCUPS

Let's start with your biggest hurdles when it comes to effective business writing. Do you overwrite or just skip through puddles of information? Maybe you have a hard time organizing your thoughts so you fall back on stream of consciousness. Or do you struggle with the right tone for your audience? The list of possible hiccups is endless.

Unfortunately, those hiccups could be standing between you and success. The way you write determines how well you can sell yourself, your company, your product and/or your service.

In fact, your written materials may be the only opportunity you have to engage your target audience, internally and/or externally.

- An effective letter, email, memo, report or executive summary can capture and keep your reader's attention.

- An ineffective communications can push your reader right into the clutches of a competitor.

But If It's Worked Well Enough So Far?

Here's the reality when it comes to written communications.

- No one wants to read what you've written.

- Almost no one will read all of it.

- Almost everyone will misunderstand some part of it.

Further, that tide of information coming at your reader is growing. Rapidly. There is a reason soft skills and quality communications continue to spark article after article on the importance of strengthening how you write to your audience. So, no, you can't keep plodding along. It's time to make a change.

INFORMATION DELUGE

It's 7:00 a.m. There's the alarm followed by radio voices alerting you to the latest news. TV commentators accompany you as you dress, only to be replaced by a wide array of verbal and digital iPad/computer/phone headlines as you segue to breakfast. Even before you get to your workspace, you've already hit overload.

How much overload? The figures are daunting.

- In every two-day period, we generate as much information as man did from the dawn of civilization until the year 2003.

- The majority of us have the equivalent of half a million books on our computers. That's enough to fill a library.

- Basically, the human brain is receiving 34 GB of information on a daily basis.

It's a virtual avalanche of input coming at us, an avalanche you are about to contribute to, expecting your readers to stop what they are doing and consider what you've written. Your business letters, emails, reports, position papers, memos – everything you create that requests action on your reader's part will be competing with every other piece of information coming across that reader's desk.

Your recourse? Some writers opt just to add more information. Surely the reader will succumb and absorb a portion of the volume of words on that email, text or page. Dream on.

- When we go to an Internet page we choose to go to, we typically spend 58 seconds.

- When it comes to email, estimates put the reader's attention at 11 seconds.

- To assume the reader is going to spend more time than that on your document is naïve.

How are you going to change the way you produce anything written to capture your reader's attention more effectively? By breaking through the information swamping your targeted audience. By taking the puzzle apart and putting it back together differently. You are going to start thinking, organizing and generating relationship-driven writing.

It's not easy. But it's worth it. The more you use these new techniques, the more you change your behavior, the fewer follow-up phone calls and emails in your future. Your communications will begin to more effectively drive the reader to accomplish your goals.

Good News

Writing is like anything else. The more you practice, the better you get. And, the better you are as a writer, the more you begin to differentiate yourself in the workplace.

> *Grammar Note: Notice that sentence started with "and"? The grammar gods and goddesses decreed we can start sentences with "and," "but," "because" and "however." We can't start paragraphs with those words, but we can start sentences.*

> *That said, introducing a sentence with "and," "but," "because" and "however" really is a style issue. It does not add to your message. Rather, it shows an aspect of your personality. Be cautious though. In the business world, some readers will view your starting sentences with those words as a grammatical faux pas. You are probably*

best served saving "and," "but," "because" and "however" for creative writing opportunities.

After all, isn't that what you're all about? Standing out as being better at what you do so you are recognized for that new opportunity, that new project, that new job.

Writing Is Just Like Speaking

Writing of any kind is just like speaking, but you are sitting on the other side of the screen, the other side of a piece of paper. You don't have the luxury of:

- Pausing to make sure your audience is getting the information.

- Rephrasing in response to that glazed look in his eyes.

- Telling her a joke to keep her attention.

- Touching him on the shoulder to yank him back to reality.

> **Writing, when properly managed, is but a different name for conversation.**
> *— Laurence Sterne, English novelist*

Consequently, your writing has to be:

- Interesting.

- Informative.

- Personal.

Why personal? Think about it. What happens when you choose a restaurant? Usually you opt for one where, beyond the food itself, staff listen to your desires, take your order and care about your reactions. Likewise when you go shopping. You choose a store that provides a welcoming level of customer service.

The same holds true in the workplace. Your buyers have numerous companies with which they can do business. Your managers have a roster of employees from which they can select to staff a project. Those "clients" are going to choose the person with whom they can envision a working relationship.

No More Formality

Growing up, we were taught writing should be very formal.

- Dear Mr. Jones followed by a colon.

- Justified left and right margins.

- All those multi-syllable words you practiced for the next vocabulary quiz.

We tended toward formality. So much so that, somewhere along the way, business writing came quite close to mirroring that of the legal profession's style. That no longer works. (Is anyone, save another lawyer, motivated to read a legal document, much less take action?).

This means dropping formality. Today we replace the colon after "Dear Mr. Jones" with a comma. Often we have ragged right margins, and lean toward words more easily understood. We can't afford to push our reader away with formality.

Always In Sell Mode

Why is that important? Because when you write, you are in sell mode. You are selling your message, your product, your service and your thought process, even if it is as subtle as "I'm on top of things."

What's going to make you more effective at achieving that result is building a relationship with your audience so you keep the reader's attention long enough to sell your recommendation, your call to action, your information.

> **Writing crystallizes thought and thought produces action.**
> — *Paul J. Meyer, Pioneer of the Self-Improvement Industry*

Streamlining And Simplifying

Ever read something chock full of long, pretentious sounding words and wondered, "Just what am I reading?"

Read the paragraph below. Oh, go ahead. Read it out loud. Nobody is listening, and you'll get far more out of these exercises if you hear as well as see the information.

The management of this company, after due and careful consideration of certain regrettable practices which have recently been brought to our attention, is desirous of again directing to your cerebral cognizance for consequent contemplation the fact – which has, of course, been pointed out on several previous occasions but which nevertheless has apparently been overlooked or ignored by an all-too preponderant proportion of our present personnel – that

all members of this firm should make an earnest, sincere, continuous, and persistent effort to eschew and avoid all excessive lexical expressions, repetitive phraseology, unnecessarily complicated syntax, and lengthy, involved, or obfuscating paragraphs in the process of transmitting internal communication of any nature whatsoever to one or more recipients within the corporate context.

> That's not writing, that's typing.
> — *Truman Capote, Author*

Terrifying isn't it? Note that's all one run on sentence!

Too many big words, too many words at all can repel your reader. It's all about streamlining and simplifying your writing.

Too Many Words

Despite the fact that the time required for the improvement of one's writing skills may seem excessive at the beginning, it will pay dividends in the long run, for once a reasonable degree of skill in writing is achieved, it will be apparent the time needed in the future to write will be appreciably less.

That said something about writing, didn't it? But your reader isn't motivated to go back and reread it to get the message. Plus she has other emails, communications and tasks competing for her attention. To be effective, streamline to get the reader's attention and get your message across.

Streamlined and Simplified

At first it will seem to take forever to improve your writing skills. However, your investment will pay off. Your future writing will need much less effort.

Your reader has it on the first pass. It's basically the *USA Today* approach to communications.

When *USA Today* was introduced in the 1980s, people referred to it as the "Mc" paper. It had short articles, lots of color, and gave just enough of the story to interest readers. Critics' comments? *USA Today* was fine for the common man, but senior executives and decision-makers were still going to turn to *The Wall Street Journal* and the *New York Times* for their information.

Well, P.S., in 2007, *The Wall Street Journal* and the *New York Times* reformatted their publications to more closely emulate *USA Today*. Those management teams realized senior executives, decision-makers, all kinds of people want shorter amounts of information in more easily understood phrases. Audiences of every profile are after immediate applicability.

Streamlining Into Confusion

Unfortunately, some writers assume mastering streamlining means, "Let me type really quick and get out of the way." As a result, you have the following real examples from Fortune 500 Company managers:

- **What I need is a list of specific unknown problems we will encounter.**

- **Email is not to be used to pass on information or data. It should be used only for company business.**

- **As of tomorrow, employees will only be able to access the building using individual security cards. Pictures will be taken next Wednesday, and employees will receive their cards in two weeks.**

- **This project is so important, we can't let things that are more important interfere with it.**

- **We know that communication is a problem, but the company is not going to discuss it with the employees.**

So streamline to simplify, but make sure not to lose the message in the process.

BUILDING A FOUNDATION

Okay, don't panic. We are going to start with a few simple, expeditious, rewarding steps. Namely, what can we cut for immediate conciseness?

Unnecessary Prepositional Phrases

Get rid of unnecessary prepositional phrases. Fewer words on the page means more blank space. More blank space increases readability.

> Rather Than: members of the IT committee
>
> Use: ~~members of the~~ IT committee

Those of you who would have used "IT committee members," stop and think. Is the word "members" necessary?

The most valuable of all talents is that of never using two words when one will do.
— *Thomas Jefferson, American Forefather*

Wordy Modifiers

Remember how teachers said to write, "Paint a picture. Make the reader feel like she's in the room with you." Today's reader doesn't want to be in the room. She's barely interested in looking in the door.

Instead, delete words that mean the same as the word they modify.

Rather Than: he smiled happily

Use: he smiled ~~happily~~

Rather Than: advance planning

Use: ~~advance~~ planning

You hear it all the time. "He quickly ran." "Let's do it over again." It's habit. It's the way we have always done it. Your new goal is to decrease the number of unnecessary words on the page.

Obvious Adjectives

If we like modifiers, we are crazy about adjectives. Get rid of the redundant adjectives.

Rather Than: big ocean

Use: ~~big~~ ocean

After all, when was the last time you saw a small ocean?

> **Rather Than:** past history
>
> **Use:** ~~past~~ history

Ever hear yourself saying "a loud crash," or "give me the basic fundamentals"? Again, it's habit. We have to break that habit.

What else do we have to stop using for conciseness?

Buzzwords

Buzzwords (and acronyms) are vernacular that makes sense to those in a particular work environment, but not necessarily to the reader (or even your manager).

> *A group of rheumatologists with whom I was working told me, "You have to interdigitate the muscles for women who have osteoporosis." The rheumatologists meant you had to knead the muscles together to give the women relief. Later I took a brush-up Bridge course from a rocket scientist who wanted me to interdigitate the cards. He meant shuffle. Given their use of buzzwords, I had a hard time following what these guys meant.*

By using buzzwords or acronyms, you run the risk of losing your reader. The minute you lose your reader, there goes your opportunity to communicate. For instance:

Downtime.

What does downtime mean to you? Free time? Vacation time?

> The word "downtime" was developed in the manufacturing environment to represent billable time

lost when a piece of equipment is not working. So say you are talking to someone whose system is not working and she refers to downtime. If you reply, "How nice. Where are you going?" you've lost that reader's attention.

Skill Set.

What is someone's skill set? It's what they do, right?

Years ago we tacked "wise" onto everything. Time wise, height wise, size wise. Eventually we dropped the word "wise" because it added nothing to the sentence. These days, we are fixated on adding "set" onto everything. Skill set, solution set, risk set. Be the first on your block to drop it. It will probably go the way of "wise" in the not too distant future.

Bandwidth.

Do you use the phrase "bandwidth"?

There are people out there who don't follow technical jargon. When you type bandwidth, FaceTime or similar words adopted from the world of technology, there are readers who will not follow. Someone actually said to me the "net net net of the situation." I still have no idea what that person was referring to.

Grammar Note: Notice the "to" at the end of the sentence above? Despite the frowns of grammar school teachers, past and present, you can now end sentences with prepositions if doing otherwise would make the sentence off-putting. As Winston Churchill said, "That is a situation up with which I cannot put." The good news is 95 percent of the time you can rewrite and avoid ending in that preposition.

What Else Do You Avoid?

The Unnecessary That Or Which

Are you one of the many people who add "that" to a sentence? Like you are trying to thumbtack the sentence on the page with unnecessary words?

> **Rather Than:** I knew that she left the conference room.
>
> **Use:** I knew ~~that~~ she left the conference room.

> **Rather Than:** Empty the shredder that contains the report.
>
> **Use:** Empty the shredder ~~that contains the report~~.

In reality, we don't care what's in the shredder. It's shredded!

When you proof your copy, search for "that" and then determine if it adds to the sentence. You will find it is, more often than not, unnecessary.

> *Grammar Note: There is a difference between "that" and "which." The word "that" precedes information necessary to the sentence. "Which" introduces phrases complementary to the sentence.*

Southern barbecue that is made with mustard and vinegar is popular in Georgia and Alabama.

We have to be aware of the mustard and vinegar to understand what Southern barbecue is.

Southern barbecue, which can be served on fine China or paper plates, is popular in many major cities.

We don't have to consider the fine China or paper plates to understand what Southern barbecue is. Consequently, phrases beginning with "which" are bracketed by commas as those phrases can be dropped without hurting the sentence.

The Unnecessary "A" Or "The"

Ever notice how some British or Canadian speakers might say, "I'm going to hospital"? They often omit articles when they speak. Southerners and those learning English as a second language often go in the opposite direction, sprinkling in an extra "a," "an" and "the."

Rather Than:	**What kind of a program are you planning?**
Use:	**What kind of a~~ program are you planning?**
Rather Than:	**The CEO assumes the responsibility for his actions.**

> **Use:** **The CEO assumes ~~the~~ responsibility for his actions.**

This is not to advocate against "a," "an" or "the." It's simply to remind you fewer words on the page increase readability. If those articles are not necessary, why include them? Again, it's about changing habits.

Notice how we are moving toward more concise writing? These are simple steps, steps that will make a difference and decrease the words on page. What else?

Redundant Writing

The reader is going to allot you only the most finite attention. You do not have the latitude of redundant/repetitive writing.

> **Rather Than:** **Submitting three references is a necessary requirement.**

We don't have unnecessary requirements. Submitting three references is either necessary or required.

> **Rather Than:** **Merge the documents together.**

Once the documents are merged, they will be together. Again, it goes back to the language we heard growing up. "Pour ingredients in the beaker together." "Stir the batter together."

We've heard similar phrases all our lives. Time to start breaking those habits.

Redundant Phrases

If we like redundant writing, we are crazy about redundant phrases.

Rather Than:	Use:
In order to	To
Due to the fact that	Because
With regard to	Regarding or About
In the event that	If

Take "in the event that." You can almost see the writer standing arms akimbo. "In the event that" distances you from your reader. Using the word "if" is more approachable and brings the reader in.

You are trying to create relationships. Redundant phrases like "as per our conversation," "therefore," etc. as well as those above push your reader away.

So What Can You Use?

That was a lot of what not to do. What do you use when writing?

Use Of The Word "You"

Use information that draws the reader in. This means ample use of the word "you."

> **Rather Than:** As CIO, I am responsible for overall operations and don't interact with the staff in charge of the department that will supply you with the details you have requested. I am forwarding your letter to Jane Doe who will be better able to handle it.

What is the message being sent to the reader? Basically, "get out of my hair," right? "Leave me alone." "I am much too busy." Instead:

> **Use** In your letter of June 9, you requested statistics acquired from our recent survey. Survey results are coordinated by our Research Department under the supervision of Jane Doe, Director. I have forwarded your letter to Ms. Doe and asked her to respond directly to you. Please contact Ms. Doe at 404.555.5555 if you do not receive a response within the next two weeks.

Yes, the copy is longer, but look what we've done:

- Clarified this is not a form letter.

- Acknowledged the date of the reader's communications and repeated her concern. In other words, we've told the reader we heard her. Often, that acknowledgement alone helps diffuse the situation.

- Included a little public relations on how we handle similar requests.

- Given the reader next steps – whom to call, when to call and how to call.

Is that reader off our desk? Have we kept the reader as client? Yes and yes. By writing to the reader to accomplish your goal, you become the more effective writer.

> **The skill of writing is to create a context in which other people can think.**
> — *Edwin Schlossberg, American designer, author, artist*

Goal Driven Wording

Equally important is goal driven wording.

| Rather Than: | I'd appreciate it if you'd forward the list of new employees as soon as possible. |

How quickly do you think you are going to get that list of new employees? Maybe when your request gets to the top on the third pile on the left side of the reader's desk – if you are lucky. Instead:

Use: **Can you forward the list of new employees to me by 3 p.m. Wednesday so I can complete the organizational directory by Friday?**

Yes, there are still some people who will not respond. But you've increased your chances of getting a response by reminding the reader you two are in this together. You are not implying your work is more important than his. Further, you've given the reader everything he needs to respond: when you need it, why you need it and how you need it.

Passive Vs. Active Voice

Remember the difference between passive and active voice? Using passive voice, the action is done to the subject. Active voice empowers the subject to do the acting.

Passive voice: **The motivational speech was attended by the administrative staff.**

Active voice: **The administrative staff attended the motivational speech.**

We speak in active voice. Good books are written in active voice. Technical papers today are written in active voice. It is more interesting. It keeps the reader's attention longer.

You should be changing passive voice to active voice at least 80 percent of the time. In fact, the only reason to use passive voice is to describe the past or shift the blame.

Rather Than: **Sidney levied a fine on Carey for being the last person in the room.**

Use: **A fine was levied on Carey for being the last person in the room.**

With passive voice, we don't know who levied the fine. In the reference section of this book, you'll find articles on how to use your PC or Mac for assistance in tracking passive voice sentences.

The Be Verb

Strong voice, strong verbs. Get rid of that boring "be," "is," "are," "was" – those "be" verbs we lean on constantly. There are over one million words in the English language, and we are adding 450 words a year. In fact, we have three times the number of words of any language on earth.

As an adult, you typically 'own' between 70,000 to 80,000 words. This means you have other words in your vocabulary to replace "is," "are," "be," etc. Using more interesting, stronger verbs increases the draw of your sentence.

For instance, "the cherry is tart" is a ho-hum sentence. Replace that sentence with "the tart cherries made Geri's mouth pucker," and you've grabbed the reader's attention as well as provided more information. Take a look at an example.

Rather Than:	**The airline executives are unwilling to forgo their bonuses this year despite economic pressures being experienced by the airlines.**
Use:	**Airline executives decline to forgo this year's bonuses despite economic pressures affecting the airline industry.**

By indicating that the airline executives decline or refuse to forgo this year's bonuses, haven't I made the sentence more interesting and given you more details? Meanwhile, the economic pressures aren't just being experienced by the airlines, they are having an impact. By replacing the "be" verb with a more interesting verb, I've kept your attention longer.

Word To The Wise

Speaking of "affecting the airline industry," remember the difference between affect and effect? Most people get the two confused. We affect an effect.

Your trick is "affect" begins with "A" which is action so it's a verb. "Effect," which begins with an "E," is a noun 90 percent of the time. Does it matter if you use the wrong word? Yes! If your readers are attentive to correct word usage, your incorrect word choice could cost you their attention to what you wrote and their respect for your brand.

The website http://public.wsu.edu/~brians/errors/errors.html clarifies the difference between council and counsel, farther and further, capital and capitol, and much more — those words that cause most of us difficulty. Bookmark it. Then take the extra few seconds to jump over to decide if you are right as you write.

Make Those Verbs Concise

As long you are replacing "be" with more interesting verbs, make sure those verbs are concise. Streamline the verbs below, covering up the list on the right side as you answer.

Instead of	**Try:**
Seek acquisition	Acquire/Get
Render assistance	Assist/Help
Come to a conclusion	Conclude/End
Engage in a discussion	Discuss/Talk
Offer an estimation	Estimate
Give indication	Indicate

See the difference? Making your verbs concise also translates to fewer words on the page. Fewer words mean increased readability.

Apostrophes

Do you notice the typo in the box to the right? "You'r" should be "you're" or "you are." Misuse of the apostrophe is one of the top

20 grammatical mistakes most of us make.

Apostrophes signal either:

- Contraction.

- Possession.

Since contractions rarely surface in business writing, your use of apostrophes most often will indicate possession. Yet,

- If I am talking about ABC's of the situation, is that possessive? No, but we invariably put an apostrophe before the "s." (Should be ABCs.)

- If I ask you about the SKU's in inventory, are they possessive? No, but people put that apostrophe before the "s" almost every time. (Should be SKUs.)

- Those signs on the interstate showing houses in the $200's? They are grammatically incorrect. (Should be $200s.)

Now which of these signs are correct?

My favorite is the one on the bottom. The person creating this sign hedged his bets. One of these had to be correct!

Back To Writing Tips

Institutional Writing

Remember very formal writing can easily alienate your reader, motivating her to turn to another communications. Instead of using institutional style writing, refocus on relationship-driven writing. Take a look at this:

Rather Than: In accordance with suggestions embodied in your memorandum of February 22, issuance of a supplement to the April report was hence undertaken. Two (2) copies of the aforementioned supplement are enclosed herewith for your information and records. We beg to express our gratitude for your thoughtful suggestion and hope that you give forthcoming reports the same kind of carefully conceived consideration.

Overwhelming isn't it? You are never going to write to this person again for fear of the resources she would expend writing you back. Instead consider something like:

Use: On February 22, you suggested we issue a supplement to the April report. Here are two copies of that supplement. Thank you for your suggestions.

Tada! By rephrasing the same information and in half the space, it becomes clear we are both appreciative and approachable.

Grammar Note: Take a look again at the "Rather than." See the "Two (2)"? This infers the reader is too stupid to grasp what "two" stands for. Further, in the

> *financial world, numbers in parentheses are negative, so we are giving the reader two copies and taking two copies back. He gets none.*
>
> *The grammar rule is spell out single digit numbers – one through nine. Express double-digit numbers in integers. This is, unless your organization's writing guidance specifies otherwise. Your company style guide always overwrites any of the rules offered here.*

Look again at the second sentence in the example above. It begins with the word "two" spelled out. If the sentence had begun with 48, the opening "48" would have to be spelled out because, in grammar world, that's how numbers at the beginning of sentences are presented.

What if your reader is moving through your copy when, three or four sentences in, he arrives at a sentence that begins, "Forty-eight hours ago"? In that nanosecond, like a Pavlovian response, the reader is transported to grammar school where the teacher is intoning, "Numbers at the beginning of sentences must be spelled out." He remembers the smell of the classroom, maybe even the kid who always threw spitballs, before shaking himself back to reality.

It happens so fast, it happens so often, we aren't aware of its happening. But the damage is done. The reader has lost his train of thought, forgotten what he was reading before tripping down Memory Lane. Is he going to go back and reread the copy that came before? Of course not. He is going to plow forward, mentally paraphrasing what he thought he had read.

As a grammatically correct writer, spell out numbers at the beginning of sentences. As an effective writer, avoid starting sentences with numbers.

Wordiness And Clichés

Avoid wordiness and clichés.

> **Rather Than:** **This is to acknowledge receipt of the suggestions you sent pursuant to our conversation regarding the office modifications. Please be advised that we are keeping our options open at this time. We gratefully acknowledge your attention to this matter.**

You wouldn't walk up to a friend and say, "Pursuant to our conversation, where would you like to go to lunch?" Then why write that way? You are better served using something like:

> **Use:** **The office remodeling suggestions you submitted arrived on November 10. We are reviewing our options and will let you know if the committee decides to move ahead.**

With which company in these examples would you prefer working? The company responding with the "use" example comes across as a far more appealing client.

Negativity

No matter what your mood or level of frustration, replace negative copy with positive copy whenever possible. As a human being, if you come at me swinging, I'm going to dig my heels in and get ready to swing back. Approach me with dignity and respect, and I'm more apt to listen to you. It really comes down to treating other people the way you like to be treated. Take a look.

Rather Than: **If you do not respond by the end of the week, we will not fill your order.**

In the example above, no one wins. The customer doesn't get what she wants, and you don't get her business. Rephrased below, the sentence still indicates the consequences of non-action, but keeps the door open.

Use: **Please contact us by the end of the week with the information required so we can respond to your order.**

Remember, you aren't in this person's world. She may have been unable to prioritize responding to this order for any number of reasons. By leaving the door open, by leaving the customer her dignity, you keep the possibility of building a business relationship.

Please Decrease Your Pleases

Look at the word "Please" in the example above. "Please" does two things: it gives the reader the option of not following through, and it puts you, the writer, in a subservient position.

For most of us, "yes sir," "no ma'am," "please" and "thank you" are in our very bones. Unfortunately, we have carried these habits into the business world often to our detriment. Think about the people you admire, the mentors, the teachers, and the leaders. When presenting a new possibility, they don't say, "I have a new idea. Will you please take care of that and if you do that thank you maybe we can make this work."

Instead they say, "Let's try this new idea. You check on that area, you do such and so, and we'll get back together and see how it works." That kind of language assigns equal responsibility, puts everybody on the same level, and accords respect. It shows leadership. When you use "please," you fail to demonstrate you can hold your own, take responsibility, or do what needs to be done.

Look at the sentence again. How can we change it so you are not begging for a response?

Rather Than:	**Please contact us by the end of the week with the additional information required so we can respond to your order.**
Consider:	**If you contact us by the end of the week with the information required, we can respond to your order.**
Or	**Can you contact us by the end of the week with the information required so we can respond to your order?**

Either option keeps the door open while still showing respect. The "please" version does nothing for you.

You are hereby limited to only one "please" per document, and it cannot be in your first or your last sentence. (There are still some readers for whom you need to use please: older readers, people of more formal cultures, etc. Consider the reader but look for ways to practice showing your managerial chops as opposed to "begging.")

Thank You

The same holds true of the phrase "thank you." Do you automatically end your emails with the phrase "thank you"? So your email might read, "Jump off the roof, thank you" or "You're fired, thank you."

Alternatives to that close to your email will be reviewed later. For now, start monitoring your overuse of "please" and "thank you." It's about showing your professional self.

Hope, Feel, Believe

More professional positioning extends to revisiting the words "hope," "feel" and "believe."

Were I to write, "I hope you will benefit," your immediate reaction is, "You mean I might not?" Similarly writing "We believe this will affect" will make your reader wonder, "Don't you know?"

Replace those with more affirming statements.

Rather Than:	I hope you will benefit . . .
Use:	You will benefit

> **Rather Than:** We believe this will affect
>
> **Use:** This will affect

If you need your caveats, replace "This will affect" with something like "The majority of our clients find this affects."

Specific Details As Opposed To Vagueness

Replace vagueness with specific details. Were I to email a group of future class participants that class will be running late that day, most likely I will get back numerous emails asking, "How late?" or even "Should I bring my sleeping bag?" (We human beings always assume the worst.) Instead, give specifics when they are available.

> **Rather Than:** Slightly behind schedule
>
> **Use:** One day late
>
> **Rather Than:** Very overspent
>
> **Use:** Overspent by $1000

Don't want to indicate how much the budget is over or how far behind schedule you are? Then certainly avoid the details, but get ready for additional emails and/or phone calls.

The Obvious

Finally, replace the obvious with more expedient wording.

> **Rather Than:** I personally think
>
> **Use:** I think

After all, whom else do you think for?

Rather Than: **Your letter was received**

Use: **Recently you wrote**

Obviously you received the letter. Why would you write back otherwise? Rather than, "Your letter was received," try "On June 5, you wrote," and use it for extra clarity. Again get rid of the obvious and be more streamlined in your writing.

YOUR TURN

Revise these 21 words down to 8 or 9:
(Revised answer in reference section.)

> **It was a 20-minute period of time after the accident had occurred when the emergency vehicles arrived to lend assistance.**

_____

_____

• Have nine words? Take a look at your first word. Do you need it?

• Did you start with the word 20? You had to spell it out, running the risk of losing your reader's attention.

Try again. Remember your goal is active voice, which means present tense. Make sure you're talking about what has really happened.

Revise the following 21 words down to 12:
(Revised answer in reference section.)

It was decided that the club would organize a committee for the purpose of conducting a search for a new leader.

_____

_____

Did you indicate the club had already organized the committee? If I wanted to be on that committee and read that, I'd be very upset.

By The Numbers

> **Vigorous writing is concise. A sentence should contain no unnecessary words, a paragraph no unnecessary sentences, for the same reason that a drawing should have no unnecessary lines and a machine no unnecessary parts.**
> — *William Strunk, Jr., author of The Elements of Style*

Ultimately we are striving for conciseness. So your new rules of thumb are:

- Restrict business sentences to no more than 15 to 20 words. Some sentences can have three words, some eight, but top off at no more than 15 to 20.

  Why? Your reader can take in 100 percent of an eight-word sentence. He can take it 80 percent of a

12-word sentence. Over 15 to 20 words, and the reader forgets the beginning of the sentence by the time she gets to the end.

- Limit hard copy business paragraphs to no more than seven to nine lines. Note that is lines, not sentences. Go over nine lines, and the reader is mentally repelled by the volume of copy before he even begins reading.

- Reduce electronic business paragraphs to no more than three to four lines per paragraph. The reader looking at a computer screen is already scanning the text. Even more of a challenge, over 60 percent of your electronic messages will be read on a hand held device. This means the reader is going to start scrolling within the first few lines. Longer paragraphs will not be read.

THE WRITING PROCESS

Now you have tools to improve conciseness, decluttering, and specificity, but there is still a blank screen sitting in front of you. It's time to address the actual writing process.

Write To The Reader

Before you ever lay fingers to keyboard or pencil to paper, stop and think about your reader.

- Who is your reader? Effective relationship-driven writing is all about writing to the reader.

- What is that reader's attitude? Is he on your side or against you? Translation: do you have to do some additional song and dance to get his attention?

- How much time will the reader spend on this? Will he scan it or give it the two minutes you're hoping for?

- Is he the only reader? Will he be passing this up the food chain to his supervisor or on to others?

- What does the reader need to know? Not what do you need to tell him, but what does he need to know to take the action you are hoping to motivate?

Get It Together

Next, gather the information you need to compose your written communications. If you start typing, you may suddenly remember something else that should be included. Try to cram that into your message, and it's going to look like you tried to cram it in.

Organize Your Thoughts

Do you organize your thoughts before you start writing? That organizational step should be 30 percent of the writing process. Over the next few weeks, while you are breaking in new habits, try MAP-ping.

MAP: Message Audience Purpose

Write out your Message
- What's your major point in one sentence?

- What one thing do you want the audience to remember?

Identify your Audience
- Who are they?

- What is the relationship you are building?

List your Purposes (Just list them. You can reorder afterwards.)
- What do you have to convey/accomplish?

- What are your calls to action/recommendations/ good will?

Use keywords/key phrases. This seemingly extra step will expedite the amount of time you spend writing, decrease the amount of time you spend editing, and keep you on point when you do write.

> *Note: Map-ping is not something you need to do on every document or email you prepare. Writing to a colleague or someone with whom you have an on-going relationship? Clearly, map-ping isn't necessary. It will*

prove beneficial, however, when you are creating a message for an important or prospective internal or external client.

There is a second benefit to map-ping. As you train your mind to order your thoughts prior to writing, you begin training yourself to order those thoughts prior to speaking. We write like we speak. Ever noticed those folks who talk a great deal also generate copious written material? Train your brain to organize your thoughts and improve both communications skills.

Create Your Draft

- Prepare your introduction. Remember you are writing to the reader and the reader's needs.

- Structure the body of your draft with concise and streamlined copy.

- Conclude with a call to action. If you're writing to inform, this call to action is basically generating goodwill. ("If I can be of further help, contact me.") If you are writing to persuade, your closing sentences point to your recommendation. ("This report could make a difference in your planning process.) If you are writing to get the reader out of his chair to do something, your closing comments are a call to action. ("Remember the deadline is this Friday.")

It's a sandwich. It opens with what matters to the reader and closes with what matters to you. The "meat" in middle is any explanatory information needed (and only that which is needed).

Note: This "sandwich" is founded on writing to Americans. Other cultures may require a more formal or a different structure.

Remember These Pointers

Stay On Focus. I had a wonderful client who described things in extreme detail. If she wanted to tell me about her new coffee table, she started by describing the light switch on the wall. Then she moved to the wallpaper, the picture over the sofa, all before she got to the new coffee table.

Your reader isn't interested in everything in the room. He barely wants to pause at the door.

K.I.S.S. If you're from the North, K.I.S.S. stands for Keep It Simple Stupid. If you're from the South, it's Keep It Simple Sweetie. K.I.S.S. is a journalistic term. Keep It Short and Simple. Just K.I.S.S. me with the information.

Watch Your Transitions. Transitions are about keeping the reader reading. That requires a lot of air around the copy, a lot of white space. Otherwise, the reader is defeated immediately simply by the amount of copy she has to read. Just by keeping your electronic paragraphs to three to four lines and your hard copy paragraphs to seven to nine lines, you are forced to transition to your next paragraph.

Don't have a transition statement? That's where a header goes. It announces to the reader, "I am about to change subjects."

Use White Space, Bullets, Headers And Formatting For Benefit. Brain research tells us when we walk away from the first encounter with someone, we remember only the first and last comments he made.

The same is true when we look at copy on the screen or a piece of paper the first time. Our eye goes to the top of the screen/page looking for the start. We then do this censorship scan down the page looking for the end, looking for air. Typically this takes us to the bottom of the page.

So, in this preliminary censorship scan, your reader captures your first couple of lines and your last couple of lines. She uses that information sample to assess how important the information is to her, how much time she is going to have to spend on it, how interested she is in reading it now, etc.

It's like an ad in a magazine. When you encounter an ad that is copy heavy, you are apt to turn away. If, however, the ad is laid out with lots of white space, bullets and short phrases, you will probably scan it, maybe even read it.

If graphic artists are paid to create that attention-getting look, why not take advantage of those "selling" techniques in your business communications? When you are creating your document, electronically or in hardcopy, use bullets. Use headers. Keep your copy short. Then as the reader scans down the page, his eye gets caught by the air under the header and the white space beside the bullets. He reads a little more of your copy in the first scan. The result? You get a leg up pre-selling your message.

Start As Few Paragraphs With "I" As Possible. And "I" is the same as "we," "our," or your organization's name. By starting with "I," you make your message about you, not your reader. You indicate your needs are more important than those of the reader. "Stop doing what you were doing and take care of me (writer)." In fact, the next time you open an email or get a letter, notice how your hackles rise when the communication starts with "I."

For example, think about a letter you might receive selling HVAC services. The advertisement arrives stating ABC Company can clean your air conditioner better than its competitors. You know it is sales oriented from the get-go. Destination? Trash.

What if the communications started off with "Dreading the hot weather ahead?" Or even "When was the last time you had your AC checked?" Now the communications is about you, the reader. If it resonates with you and your pain, you are more apt to keep reading.

Years ago, I joined a local botanical garden. Two weeks later, a letter arrived from that attraction. The opening sentences of that letter were something like, "We are so glad you joined the gardens. We are one of the top attractions here in the city. We have so many activities you and your family will enjoy."

My response? I put the letter down. I had already joined the gardens. Why did I need to read more sales material? If the letter had begun, "Imagine spending the next rainy afternoon in our orchid conservatory." or "Have you thought about having a meeting in your rose garden?" I might have kept reading.

Take a look.

> **I like your opinion piece on the challenges facing millennials today, and the specifics between Generation Y and Generation Z. I definitely see a marketing approach that could capture a new audience for our product. I am going to suggest it to our marketing team, and I'm sure it will be put into the planning process. I'll share your opinion piece with the staff assigned to spearhead the collateral development. And I'll make sure you get credit for your work. I think this was a novel thought process.**

Just count the number of "I" placements alone.

> **_I_ like your opinion piece on the challenges facing millennials today, and the specifics between Generation Y and Generation Z. _I_ definitely see a**

> marketing approach that could capture a new audience for our product. _I_ am going to suggest it to our marketing team, and _I_'m sure it will be put into the planning process. _I_'ll share your opinion piece with the staff assigned to spearhead the collateral development. And _I_'ll make sure you get credit for your work. _I_ think this was a novel thought process.

You have to wonder if you are even going to get credit for your research, right?

What if the note read:

> **Your opinion piece on the challenges facing millennials today was excellent. Including specifics across Generation Y and Generation Z also underscored key differences. This piece could spark a marketing approach that captures a new audience for our product.**
>
> **I am going to share this with our marketing team and foresee the piece's becoming essential to the planning approach. You will get full credit throughout development.**
>
> **You came up with a very novel thought process. Let's discuss other areas you are interested in exploring.**

Not only is the copy broken into more easily read paragraphs, it is about you, the reader.

> **<u>Your</u> opinion piece on the challenges facing millennials today was excellent. Including specifics**

across Generation Y and Generation Z also underscored key differences. This piece could spark a marketing approach that captures a new audience for our product.

I am going to share this with our marketing team and foresee the piece's becoming essential to the planning approach. You will get full credit throughout development.

You came up with a very novel thought process. Let's discuss other areas you are interested in exploring.

Yes, there is one "I" in the second paragraph. It is perfectly acceptable to use the word "I" as we did, but it is not in the first paragraph. It also appears only once in the entire communications.

See the difference? Your new marching orders are:

- Limit your use of the word "I" (we/our/company name).

- Do not use "I" in your first sentence. This also applies to the implied "I" such as "As a valued customer." (You are placing the value, not the reader.)

Reducing the use of "I" will be the most Herculean task in changing your business writing. (The second hardest is reducing the use of the word "please.")

Thank You.

Given I've already made your life difficult (see above), why not add to your challenges?

You've taken somebody to the airport in the middle of the night. The next day, you arrive home planning to make dinner, let the dog out, and get some work done before settling in to the television show you want to watch.

Scanning your emails, you see one from the friend you took to the airport. The email starts off with "Thanks for taking me to the airport." You know exactly what this email is about. Do you keep reading? No. It's like reading a thank you note for a gift that starts out "Thank you very much for…" You know what you gave the person. Why keep reading?

The same is true in the business world. In 75 percent of instances, an executive who receives a note or email starting with "thank you" stops reading. She assumes this is a thank you for something she has done so there is no reason to continue. As a result, that executive never arrives at your second paragraph that includes a reminder to network you with a potential client or lead.

Reformat your thank you so it gets read. Take a look:

> **Thank you for opening a checking account with Georgia Bank. We have been a trusted member of the Atlanta community for over a century.**
>
> **We meet a wide range of financial needs. For example, besides checking accounts, we offer savings accounts, rental safe deposit boxes and CDs. In addition, we provide home mortgages and home equity loans. And customers rely on us for**

on-line banking, ATM cards and credit cards, among many other services.

We are here for you, whatever your banking needs.

There are a myriad of hurdles with this letter. It:

- Starts with "thank you."

- Reads like a sales letter for something you are already participating in.

- Is all about the writer. (Count the "we" statements.)

The writer has lost the opportunity to cement your relationship with Georgia Bank further as well as tell you about additional resources available. What if the bank representative had written:

As a new Georgia Bank family checking account holder, you now have access to a wide range of financial tools including:

- **Savings Accounts**

- **Safe Deposit Boxes**

- **Loans**

Our personal bankers are available for consultation whenever you are ready to discuss your financial requirements.

Thank you for your business. We will strive to justify your confidence in us.

The bullets immediately captured your attention, right? The writer has pre-sold her message.

Beyond that, the opening sentence works to draw the reader in, and the closing paragraph still thanks the reader – but at the end of the communications. See the difference?

Think about this in terms of thank you notes for job interviews. If your follow-up note opens with "Thank you very much for," it mirrors every other thank you note the interviewer receives. Instead, start by iterating something from your meeting and end with a thank you, and you've already differentiated yourself from the other candidates.

Reread

After you've written your first draft, it's time to reread and rewrite.

- Make sure you've achieved your goal. Have you stayed on message? Look back at your MAP process to confirm you conveyed your intent.

- Streamline and declutter. Most writers can cut their copy by at least 30 percent.

- Reduce ideas to bullet points wherever possible. Readers like bullet points. Bullet points are easy to follow, increase white space on the page, and make your copy more concise.

Proof

Next,

take the time to let your copy get cold.

If you start proofing immediately, you are proofing what is in your mind, not what is on the screen. We are created, evolved, designed – whatever your personal beliefs – to read by reflected light. Computers are ambient light. We don't see what is on a screen as effectively as we see on paper. We're also reading at a faster rate.

If you don't disassociate from what you have written for some period of time – at least 20 seconds of real distraction, you are going to read what you thought you wrote, not what may be there. Get a cup of coffee. Open up a different file. Take some distance **no matter how busy you are**. Otherwise, you may well have to spend time churning out additional emails or phone calls to clarify or resolve the situation a simple typo created.

Over the next few weeks, try reading your draft out loud. This will force you to slow down and actually read what is on the screen or page, not scan, as we are more apt to do when proofing. Also, by reading aloud, you will hear your use of passive voice, where you may have left in a word you thought you took out, or how often you used the same word in one sentence or paragraph. If you won't read aloud, print your draft on recycled paper and proof it there.

(No, you don't have to do this on every piece of written material you produce. But anything going up the food chain or to an important internal or external client reflects on you. It's worth the extra few minutes to get it done right.)

As you are proofing:

- Keep in mind what your reader doesn't know. Remember your goal is to share only the information needed for the reader to take the desired action. Not everything you think the reader needs to know, might want to know, covers any question he might ask – you get the message.

- Write simply and naturally, the way you would talk. None of the "pursuant to" or "as per our conversation."

- Make your writing active – use active voice – and personal. Your goal is to create a relationship with the reader, not push her away.

- Use short paragraphs (three to four lines on electronic copy, seven to nine lines on hard copy), short sentences (15 to 20 words maximum) and short words ("try" instead of "endeavor," "change" instead of "ameliorate").

- Be specific. Get to the key information.

- Understate rather than overstate. That paragraph you keep working on only to find it keeps getting longer and longer? Delete it and start again. You were never going to get that paragraph right anyway.

- Avoid the vague adjectives, adverbs and modifiers we already addressed when discussing how to be more concise.

- Choose the correct word or your reader will notice. Plus you lose points, points you can't afford to sacrifice in this competitive environment. Remember to consult http://public.wsu.edu/~brians/errors/errors.html when you use a tricky word.

- I.e. vs. e.g. These abbreviations are not interchangeable. The abbreviation i.e., short for Id est, means "that is to say." This is a literary device that allows the writer to explain the story further. Jack went to the store, i.e., he got in his car, turned out of the parking lot and drove to Harris Teeter. As an effective business writer striving for conciseness, you should be telling the story completely the first time. There is rarely a need for i.e. in the business world.

- E.g., short for ergo, means for example. Once in the store, Jack bought groceries, e.g., dog biscuits and milk. Using e.g. does not make you look any more erudite than "including," "such as" or "for example." It is simply another option. If you do use e.g., note it is not one word. Nor does it need to appear in parenthesis.

- Compliment with an "i" versus complement with an "e". Sadly, these two spellings are confused on 50 percent of all business communications. Your trick for conquering this hurdle is to use "compliment" whenever "I" am giving the reader something: a complimentary bottle of wine, a complimentary night stay, a compliment about what a person is wearing. Use "complement" with an "e" when the goal is to indicate one thing completes the other. "The reins complement the horse's tack."

Again, visit http://public.wsu.edu/~brians/errors/errors.html when you are identifying the right word to use. Your choice matters.

Better Business Writing

Punctuate Carefully

Whether you are from the punctuation heavy school or the punctuation lite school, both are correct. Add a comma before "and" in a series or don't. Your goal is to be consistent (unless your boss has a definite preference or your organization's style guide specifies a direction).

On the subject of punctuation, a few points particular to bullets. We no longer do comma, comma and. Either put a period (or question mark, if appropriate) at the end of all of your bullets, or conclude with no punctuation at all. Go for consistency.

Grammar Note: A few grammar rules here.

- *If the bullet is a whole sentence, it has to end in punctuation.*

- *Bullets are always clones. If one starts with a verb, they all start with the verb. If one is a whole sentence, they are all whole sentences within that list.*

- *Bullets travel in a pack. You never have just one.*

- *If bullets are sequential, proceed them with "1, 2, 3" or "a, b, c." If they are of equal priority, use bullet marks.*

Comment: If you are handing out this list of bullets during a presentation, use "1, 2, and 3." It makes it easier for the audience to track the bullet you are discussing.

Make It Perfect

What I if told you
you read the top line wrong

I keep harping on rereading. Look at those extra few minutes you take to proof as an investment in your professional reputation. If someone looks at your message and finds a typo, she is going to remember that mistake longer than she remembers your message.

Double Check Phone Numbers and URLs

This is where we make our most mistakes. Giving someone a phone number? Take out the imaginary keypad and dial the number based on what you have on the screen. If you are giving multiple readers that phone number, take out the phone and call the number based on what you have on the screen. This allows you to double-check how the phone is answered and ensures you have the right number (unlike the Oregon-based company that misprinted an 800 number on the back of a cereal box sending callers to a phone sex line).

Word™ is wonderful about putting a line under a URL address and turning it a pretty shade of blue – even when there is a typo in the address. Make sure you have the correct URL.

Use Plain English Even on Technical/Medical Subjects

Do not assume your reader uses the same vocabulary you do, particularly in technical and medical environments. Even your management team may not be able to navigate the industry-specific phrases you are using in today's acronym-rich workplace.

> **When writing about science, don't simplify the science; simplify the writing.**
> — *Julie Ann Miller, former editor of Science News*

EXTERNAL COMMUNICATIONS

• Relationship-driven communications.

• The importance of writing to the reader and the reader's needs.

• The writing process.

Check, check, check. All points covered. Now it's time to apply these skills to external and internal writing projects.

Let's start with external communications, which can arrive in hard copy or via email. These communications can be used to answer inquiries, request information, ask for action, decline a request, market a product and/or a myriad of other tasks. For our discussion, the main requirement is these communications go outside of your environment.

Whichever medium you are using, hard copy or email, make sure you begin with the right name and salutation. If you do not know if Lynn is a man or woman, or spells the name with one "n" or two, and the only way to find out is to pick up the phone and call Lynn/Lyn, do so. We are very attached to our names. In fact, our good name is all we bring to the table. Use it incorrectly and lose your audience.

A young woman was a shoo-in for a job. When she wrote to the future employer, Dr. Garvy, she transposed the 'a" and the "r." When the letter arrived, Dr. Gravy turned her down. True story.

Start with the correct name or lose the reader's attention. (Particularly if the reader's name is spelled out at the bottom of the email to which you are responding!)

Think Before You Write

- Read the pertinent material and circle the point you want to address.

- Jot down the ideas you want to convey.

- Gather as much background material as necessary.

Sound familiar? It's the writing process at work.

Now Choose Your Opening Sentence Carefully

It makes the first impression – good or bad. Remember, this is what invites the reader in. The opening sentence encourages him to keep reading so get right into your message from the reader's point of view.

Unless you are conveying bad news. Then an indirect route or flipping the information where possible is the better approach. Follow this thought process.

A young man received a letter telling him he had been turned down for such and so scholarship. He wadded up the letter and threw it across the room. About a week later, he uncrumpled the letter to read it again. (For some reason, human beings like to reread bad news.) In the second paragraph, the copy stated he was an excellent candidate for a lesser-known scholarship available up to 48 hours' receipt of the letter.

Had the letter begun with "While you have been turned down for such and so scholarship, there is an excellent opportunity still available to you" or "Have you also applied for," it could have made all the difference in the young man's college opportunities.

Replying To Prior Communications?

Reference the date of that interaction in your starting sentence. This helps orient the reader and indicates clearly this is not a form letter. Yes, there may be a series of email exchanges trailing your communications, but people don't go back and read what came before. It could be as simple as "In your phone call of June 5" or "In your January 10 email."

Express The Idea Of Prime Interest To You In Your Final Sentence.

This is your call to action discussed earlier. Remember, your "sandwich." Start with what matters to the reader and end with what matters to you.

Close With The Sign-off.

That real estate, that space at the bottom of the page where we put "Regards," "Warm Regards," "Warmest Regards," "Best Regards," "Kind Regards," (at some point someone needs to explain the difference between all of those) is valuable. When your reader does her censorship scan down the page, she dismisses what looks like every other sign-off she receives.

Take advantage of that space by popping your message.

- "Looking forward to hearing from you by_____,"

- "Thank you for your interest,"

- "Let me know if you have any questions,"

Notice, I didn't write, "Please let me know if you have any questions." The "Please" does nothing for you.

Again, this works when writing to Americans. Even some Americans, those who are very formal, may require a more traditional close. You can always fall back on "Sincerely yours."

Business Letter Examples

Let's look at some business letter examples.

Original:

As a professional non-profit manager, you understand the important role associations hold in our society. That puts you in great company. Alexis de Tocqueville, the French political philosopher who spent time in America to determine what made us a great nation, thought highly of associations.

In his book, Democracy in America, de Tocqueville said that associations made American society greater than any other. Our willingness to come together for the common good - whether to build a bar or influence our government - made us special.

The State Society of Association Executives (SSAE) has been the "town center" for the profession of association management since 1901. Since then, we've been coming together to build our profession and strengthen those who practice the profession.

We do this by facilitating connections among members. As adults, we learn best from experiences. Through SSAE, our members share their successes (and, sometimes, failures) so that we can all learn from each other.

SSAE is also a source of knowledge and information about association management. We offer a variety of educational opportunities and publications that strengthen the connections we have with our profession. Through SSAE, you can grow professionally to help your association and advance your own career.

Our mission is to advance the profession while enhancing professionalism of association members. We invite you to join us on this journey by becoming a member of SSAE. Enclosed is a brochure detailing the association and its benefits to you, along with a membership application.

If you have any questions about SSAE, or if you'd just like to talk about an area of association management to get some new ideas, please feel free to call me at or email me at

This letter starts well enough. The writer talks about the reader on a positive note. Then he shares a little something about the society. From there, it's down hill. The writer introduces de Tocqueville, who gave us the foundation for government and associations, and then de Tocqueville's book. Next we hear about the association and more and more, finally ending with an invite to the reader to make contact for more information.

How many readers do you think will get all the way to the bottom of the page, much less contact the writer for more details? Few to none.

If we rephrase and reformate the letter as below, where do your eyes go?

Edited Version:

As a professional non-profit manager, you understand the important role associations hold in our society. That puts you in great company.

The State Society of Association Executives (SSAE) was formed to further our effectiveness as substantial contributors to our society. In fact, SSAE has been the "town center" for the profession of association management since 1901. For more than eight decades, we have been bringing leaders like you together to build our profession and strengthen the expertise we bring to our roles.

We do this by:

- Facilitating connections among members. Through SSAE, our members share their successes (and, sometimes, failures) so we all learn from one another.
- Serving as a source of knowledge and information about association management.
- Providing a variety of educational opportunities and publications that strengthen connections within our profession.
- Advancing the professional while enhancing professionalism of our members. This is our mission.

Join us on this journey by becoming a member of SSAE. Enclosed is a brochure detailing the association and its benefit to your organization. The brochure includes a membership application.

Contact me anytime at _____.

To the bullets, right? We have held on to the opening sentence that makes this about the reader, pre-sold our message with the bullets during the reader's censoring scan, and ended with a call to action – "Join us on this journey." If the reader is even slightly interested, she is going to invest more time reading the letter than she would have the original.

Look at another.

Original:

Gentlemen:

It was a pleasure meeting with you last week. I want to thank you for giving me the opportunity to provide accounting and tax services to your companies.

The following is a brief outline of the services that I will provide to each of your companies:

    1. I will write-up your books on a quarterly basis
    2. Prepare all quarterly payroll and applicable sales tax returns
    3. Prepare the annual corporate income tax returns
    4. I am always available to answer your questions

As I previously quoted you, I estimate my fees not to exceed $_____ per corporation. After completing the year and evaluating the time spent on your account we can revise the billings.

I will bill you on a quarterly basis.

If the foregoing is acceptable to you, please sign below and return a copy of this letter to me.

I realize you will have questions regarding this proposal, please feel free to call me. Again, I thank you for this opportunity.

Very Truly Yours,

How many mistakes can you find?

- The writer thanked the reader three times for something not yet offered.

- The bullet points are numbered and not uniform.

- The stand-alone "I will bill you" sentence stands out like a neon sign.

- If the writer realizes the reader will have questions, why send the letter?

- This is obviously a form letter.

There is nothing about the letter in the version above that sells to the reader. Revisiting the phrasing and formatting can create a more effective communications like the following version.

Edited Version:

Dear Mr. Brown:

Given the steady growth B&G's family of companies has experienced in the last two years, you are well served to identify an outside resource for your accounting and tax work. I would welcome the opportunity to supply those services as listed below:

- **Complete B&G's books on a quarterly basis**

- **Prepare all quarterly payroll and applicable sales tax returns**

- **Compile the annual corporate income tax returns**

- Serve as an on-call resource

As previously quoted, I estimate my quarterly fees not to exceed $____ per corporation. We will re-evaluate the time required to meet your accounting needs after a year of service and revise as necessary.

With the end of the year approaching, now is the time to get started. If you are ready to proceed, sign below and mail a copy of this letter back to me in the attached return envelope. Feel free to contact me with any additional questions.

Thank you for this opportunity,

In this version, the letter is personalized to Mr. Brown, capturing and keeping his attention. Bullet points are standardized and all services appear in equal value. The focus on money is lessened, and the writer has ended with a call to action – "With the end of year approaching, now is the time to get started." The one appearance of "thank you" is at the end and it is a thank you for the opportunity.

Additional samples appear next, all taken from real life examples complete with their typos and poor packaging. Take a look at each of these and think about how you would revise them before reading the possible rewrites.

Financial or Marketing Director.

I am conducting some personal research about public relations firms in your area. Could you please send me some information about your firm that includes areas of specialization, age of the firm, size of the firm, a listing of past and current clients, structure of the staff, any special resources you make use of regularly, and your general business philosophy, goals, or outlook. If available, please enclose a copy of your past two or three annual reports as well. I appreciate your assistance and look forward to receiving this information. My address is listed above. Thank you.

Possible Rewrite:

Dear Ms. Davis,

Small public relations firms like yours have clearly carved out a niche in today's economy. Our class at the University of Arizona will be studying this trend and creating a report that could prove beneficial to you as you strategize for the coming year.

If you could provide me the following information by June 1, I will return a copy of the report to you by November 30. Most particularly, comparisons would benefit from copies of any of the following as pertains to your firm:

- Areas of specialization

- Age of the firm

- Size of the firm

- A listing of past and current clients

- Structure of the staff

- Any special resources you make use of regularly

- Your general business philosophy, goals or outlook

- The last two or three annual reports

If you would like to confirm the viability of this project, feel free to contact Professor _____ (email/phone) who conducts a similar project annually.

Otherwise, get this information in by June 1. The resulting report could spell the difference in your next year's return on investment.

Dear Dr. Silver:

I have received your check in the amount of $2,276.00 and it is my understanding that you will be leasing the above property until June 30, 2020 at which time you will vacate such property

If there is any way in which I may be of further assistance, please do not hesitate to let me know. You may reach me at 653.555.9999.

Possible Rewrite:

Dear Dr. Silver:

Your check in the amount of $2,276.00 arrived confirming your occupancy of <u>address</u> through June 30, 2020. While you are here, we hope you will take advantage of the:

- Friday night parties at the pool.

- The free laundry facility on the property.

- The excellent array of dining establishments within walking distance.

Should you have any additional questions or would like to renew your lease, I can be reached at 653.555.9999.

Dear Ms. Wells,

We have reviewed your bid for the proposed project. However, we have declined your offer for the moment. We have found a company that we consider economical.

Your reputation as a contractor is excellent, and we would like to work with you in the future. We have enclosed a list of upcoming projects for you to browse through.

We look forward to hearing from you again. If you have any questions about our decision or the future projects, you contact John Doe at _____.

Possible Rewrite *Assuming You Want To Keep The Door Open:*

Dear Ms. Wells,

Your reputation as a contractor is excellent and your bid thorough. Unfortunately, budgetary restrictions dictate we select another vendor at this time.

We have enclosed a list of more flexible projects surfacing over the next six month. If you have any questions after reviewing these, feel free to contact John Doe for more information.

We look forward to working with you in the future.

Possible Rewrite *Assuming You Wish To Discourage This Vendor:*

Dear Ms. Wells,

Your reputation as a contractor is excellent and your bid thorough. Unfortunately, we have selected another vendor at this time.

Thank you for your interest,

STYLE AND TONE

Just like your words, your style and your tone are also important.

Style

Typically, when talking up the food chain, we have a tendency to be more formal. Talk to those who work for us and we are more casual. To those we do not know, the style is business-like and courteous.

So, to an equal, you might say:

> "I can't go along with the plan because I think it poses serious logistical problems."

Whereas sending the same message to a superior would look more like:

> "The logistics of moving the department may pose serious problems."

Given you do not have the time to rewrite the same message to two and three audiences, standardize on a business-like and courteous approach when writing to all audiences. That creates a style you can rely on when writing – and speaking – and takes care of any pass along of the information.

Institutional: (Too Formal/Verbose)

> Circulation cost reductions, which go into effect this month, have been made financially feasible by a recent installation of media-oriented technology.

Versus: (Too Casual)

We are cutting down on circulation costs starting this month. We couldn't have done this if we hadn't installed our new media-oriented technology.

Versus: (Business-Like, Courteous)

Circulation costs will be reduced effective this month as the result of recently installed media-oriented technology.

Tone

Tone is equally important. Ever opened a letter or email, read the copy, and thought, "that person hates me"? The tone of your communications:

- Reinforces – or threatens – the relationship with the reader.

- Is perceived as reflecting your attitude toward the reader.

- Should be conversational but not too casual.

- Provides the opportunity to downplay the negative and reinforce the positive.

Impersonal and dictatorial:

"It has been decided that the office will be open the day after Thanksgiving."

Better:

"The office will be open after Thanksgiving."

Best:

"To meet the Dec. 15th deadline for the government contract, the office will be open the day after Thanksgiving."

In other words, work on using your style and tone to build a relationship:

"Can you forward the list of new employees to me by 3 p.m. Wednesday so I can complete the organizational directory by Friday?"

INTERNAL COMMUNICATIONS

Just like external communications, internal communications are written to inform, persuade or motivate your reader. The difference is your targeted audience is inside your organization/department.

When writing to <u>inform</u> your reader, you are sending what used to be called a memo. In this vein:

- You are alerting your readers to key information, e.g., changes, updates or confirmations of which they need to be aware.

- The way you present these facts positions your readers for future interactions.

- Your goal is to strengthen their trust in and dependence on you as a source of reliable and credible information.

If you are writing to <u>persuade/motivate</u> that reader, you are asking him to change. People don't like to change. They are very happy in their ruts. Consequently, your information has to be convincing.

- Establish the need of your recommendation and support it with objective evidence.

- The way you present your ideas is as important as the ideas themselves.

- You must use basic manners in your writing that consider your reader's needs and feelings.

Emails

The vast majority of your internal communications are going to arrive via email. The email itself could arrive on a computer, a hand-held phone, an ipad or even as text to the person standing right next to you. So let's address email.

The volume of email traffic continues to grow at an explosive rate.

- In 1999, we were sending five billion emails per day.
- By 2020, we had escalated to a staggering 205 billion emails/day.

That translates to:

- 2.8 million emails/second.
- 90 trillion emails/year.

Even more wearing, over 60 percent of these emails are non-essential! As a result, you or the person to whom you are writing could be getting upwards of 400 emails in a given day. Text, data, graphics – you name it. We are sending it.

Why? Because email is thought to be the coolest, most efficient, most expedient, easiest way to communicate.

The good news about email: it is a very effective way to communicate with more than one person. No need to worry about the receiver's location, time zone or schedule. You send that email at your convenience and the receiver gets/reads the email at his.

The bad news about email: few senders think before they write. We have become so immersed in email that we seemingly are convinced what is in our heads streams out through our fingers, through the keyboard right into our reader's psyche. The resulting disconnect often causes more problems than a phone call would have. Users tend to be blunt, write stream of consciousness and leave out key elements. Consequently, recipients often miss the point, misinterpret the email and/or misunderstand.

Writing Quality Also Suffers

Email was perpetuated as a way for computer geeks to share Dungeons and Dragons moves. It was purposefully lower case, purposefully sentence fragments. Unfortunately, we have carried those same habits into the business world.

In reality, email, just like any other form of workplace correspondence should:

- Be free of:
    o Grammatical or factual errors.
    o Ambiguities.
    o Unintended implications.
- Include crucial details.

Given the possible pass along rate of emails within an organization and the almost eternal life of an email, this grammatical correctness and directness becomes even more important.

We also tend to forget:

- Emails can go places they were never meant to go. Ever sent an email to the wrong person and tried to hit recall? Yeah, right.

- Emails never die. They are alive and well on the hard drives and back-ups of our systems, even when they no longer appear on our board.

- According to the Sarbanes Oxley Act of 2002 (SOX), your employer is entitled to look at anything generated on his technology including personal interactions since he is fiscally responsible for any repercussions from those emails.

Housekeeping

You can't change the world's email habits. Nor can you change those of your organization. All you can do is begin refining your own written emails to encourage better responses and curtail your follow-up communications.

Your new golden rules are as follows:

- Restrict each message to one project/situation. If you write your reader with information and questions on three different projects, she has to edit that email so she can send it to the three different project managers involved. She also, given this email pertains to three different subjects, has to determine where to save the email file. Finally, even if she has the answers to subject questions 1 and 3, but not 2, she is not going to answer you until she has all three answers.

Don't blame her. You bundled them together. Time management tells us the best way to handle this – and get answers to your questions – is to generate three different emails to your recipient, each on a different project/situation. That way, she can quickly dash off a response and you can take action. Less finger drumming on your part.

- List only one name in the To: field. Otherwise, recipients don't recognize who holds responsibility for follow-through. This seems like a no-brainer, but you have no idea how many people will email all of their managers assuming one will step forward with a "I'll take care of that."

Include only the person (or persons) responsible to taking action in the To: field. Everyone else goes in the CC: field. By the way, BCC: is going behind the other readers' backs. Also, many BCC: recipients don't realize that, when they hit reply all, it goes to <u>everyone</u> on the list.

- Don't use emojis, emoticons or wallpaper. They may be cute, but do not denote professionalism. If this email is between you and a close friend, that's one thing. Otherwise, emojis and emoticons have no place in the business world.

Further, they may disappear on a hand-held device or show up as a   or a J. If you are depending on a smiley face to make your words less offensive, pick different words.

- Avoid acronyms. Acronyms and abbreviations are deadly enough on hard copy. On email, readers are already flying through what comes across their screens. That acronym or abbreviation can easily derail the reader's thought processes. Unless you are sure your audience is on the very same vocabulary stream you are – and that email is not apt to be passed along – avoid buzzwords and acronyms.

Opening Your Email

Email etiquette states this kind of communication is basically a memo. Because To: and From: are already there, you can omit salutations and complementary closings.

That said, the extra 10 seconds it takes you to personalize the email to the recipient helps build a relationship and capture his attention.

Omitting salutations can be beneficial when writing to a total disparate audience. What if your target group is comprised of stamp collectors, politicians and volunteers? There is no all-encompassing title for the three groups. Nor do we use "To Whom It May Concern" or "Dear Sir/Ma'am." In that instance, going straight into your message is considered acceptable.

Closing Your Email

Sign off using your personal professional preferences, but avoid:

- "Have a blessed day." Religious references are not appropriate in a business world where your preferences may differ from that of your reader. Avoid that potential offense.

- Those quotes. Once someone has read a quote, she's not really interested in seeing it again.

- Baby pictures.

Also vary those closes. Remember, this is valuable space. Make those sign-offs work. Instead of Regards or Sincerely, pop your message with phrases such as:

- Thank you for your time,

- Looking forward to hearing from you,

- See you at the 3:00 p.m. meeting,

Finally, include your return contact information at the end of all your messages. Email tends to be passed along so the ability to click through to a particular participant's email may not be possible. Further, some organizations utilize a protocol that displays the person's name as last name, first name. This, too, would not be clickable for someone who is receiving the email second or third hand.

Formatting

- Use upper and lower case. ALL UPPER CASE IS SHOUTING. All lower case worked for ee cummings, but we are not writing poetry. Be grammatically correct in your case use.

- Stick to no less than a 10-point typeface and preferably 12 point. Given your email is going to be short, the choice of typeface is less important as long as it is easily read. As far as the particular font choice, opt for something professional.

  Note: Are you aware of the difference between serif and sans serif typeface? Serif typefaces have those little artistic elements that tell the eye where to stop like

Cambria and Times Roman. Sans serif (without a serif) fonts are clean strokes that have no embellishments like Arial and Calibri.

For longer documents, select a serif typeface. The eye takes in serif type 50 percent faster than it takes in a sans serif type.

- **Cambria**   (serif preferable)
- **Arial**

- Avoid bolding, italics, font and color change. These do two things: they tell the reader nothing else on the page is important, and when they arrive on a handheld device, those visual elements usually disappear. If you want something to pop, use white space around those words instead.

- Keep your email short. Study after study tells us readers are not going to scroll down past the first page. They just are not going to do it. Further, over 60 percent of the emails you send are going to be read on a mobile device so that demands an even shorter communications.

- If your message is long, include it as an attachment and send it along with a short cover note. Yes, many people won't open an attachment, but they weren't going to open it on their cell phone anyway, nor were they going to scroll through a long email.

- Use white space. White space, air around your lines, is important on hard copy. On email, when that virtual metronome is ticking, airy copy becomes even more important. The reader needs encouragement that she can get through this email quickly and send it on its way.

- Break up text into brief paragraphs, leaving one blank line between each. Remember, we are limiting our paragraphs to three to four lines. Again, we need more air.

Preparing

About to write an email? Stop.

First:

- Gather all the information you need.
- Identify your audience.
- Outline your points.
- Use active versus passive voice.
- Use the right tone for your reader.

Sound familiar? These are the same rules we used for the writing process and for generating hard copy. Nothing has changed, save the audience.

About the audience, do not write anything you would not want other than the intended recipient to see such as:

- Confidential information.
- Criticism or reprimands.

All too often, that email could end up in the wrong hands through a mis-click, a forward or any number of reasons. One of my class participants had been emailing her best friend who was sitting right next to her. The writer was bent out of shape about a fashion risk another woman had taken that day. Guess who got the email? The woman with questionable fashion sense of course.

Writing

Your subject line is critical on emails. Studies show only some 20 percent of emails are ever read. That executive or decision maker to whom you are writing has already become inured to high priority, important or urgent flags.

To encourage your reader to open the email, make your subject line:

- Compelling. If you write something like "Insurance Reimbursement," the reader may simply forward the email to HR or Bookkeeping. If your subject line is vague like "ROI," your reader going to probably ignore what is apt to be a confusing email.

- Specific. If your subject line is "Tracking ROI on the Insurance Reimbursement Program," your reader is immediately oriented to your email's goal. He grasps what you are writing about, and that you are in control of what you are writing.

- Time driven. Need to hear from the reader by a specific time? Put that in your subject line. In fact, in a world where many readers are utilizing Outlook Preview, that time requirement needs to be one of the first three words. Otherwise, you run the risk of the email not being opened until past your deadline.

In other words, it is up to you to attract your reader. You have the room. We can type up to 78 characters in our subject line. Rarely is there a reason to include that many words, but do use the real estate to spell out what this email is about. Orient your reader. Make that subject line work.

As you are writing,

- State the most important points first. Your reader is going to start speeding through, particularly on a mobile device, so grab him while you can.

- Provide any reminders that make the reader feel an affiliation with the message. "As James mentioned on our conference call." "As Harper brought up during the meeting."

- Use your bullets and lists. These are important on hard copy. They are essential on electronic copy.

- Travel methodically through your points.

Paraphrase

Ever gotten an email that is 13 threads deep? You go to push print, and you get even more upset?

Resist the temptation to repeat the earlier message along with your response. Except in regulatory, legislative or technical environments, there are few reasons to send an email more than three threads deep. Further, no one is going to look back at email one, assess it, move to email two, etc.

Start a new email with a paraphrase of what has gone before. If that makes you nervous, cut and paste the prior emails into a file and attach it to your paraphrased email.

Oh, and change the old title on the subject line. Think about those emails that still read "Meeting" when the topic at hand is a full-scale retreat. Or those that read (Fwd:/Fwd:/Fwd/). No one is going to think, "Let me see. That was in email seven."

> *Exception: If your organization's file naming protocol is based on subject lines, keep the original subject line but add a hyphen and document what this email is about.*

Problem Solving

Disagreeing on something? After two rounds of problem solving via email, get up and walk over to the desk next to you or, if necessary, pick up the phone. You are not going to solve the problem by email. It isn't going to happen. All your reader is going to do is continue to read over that which made her angry in the first place.

Better to have an uncomfortable five minutes of one-on-one interaction to resolve the problem. Then go back to your desk and send an email indicating, "based on our discussion, you are doing this and I am doing that."

Emotions!

Beginning to get the message that email is not the end all? Before writing, consider your frame of mind.

If you are angry or irritated, get up from the computer and walk away. Stomp, kick something, distract yourself. Don't type the message and send it to draft, plan to delete it or just prepare it so you can see it in print. One of those times you are going to inadvertently press "Send" and you can't take it back.

Don't deliver bad or sensitive news in an email message. Think about how you'd like to be treated. No one deserves to learn something difficult to take via email.

We have a tendency to hide behind email. It's easy. It really comes down to the Golden Rule: treat others the way you'd like to be treated.

Don't Press Send Yet!

Over the next three weeks (remember, how long it takes to break an old habit and create a new one), stop before you press "send."

- Let your email get cold. Then reread it. You may well find yourself unpleasantly surprised at your tone, style, errors, confusion, etc. The list of errors we make when typing a quick email is endless.

- Read it slowly, even aloud if you can. Having to enunciate slows down your pace so you see what is actually on the screen. Equally beneficial, by reading aloud, you hear where you used "several" twice in the same sentence, reverted to passive voice, or didn't complete an edit you thought you had made.

- Cut the fluff. If you are like most writers, you can cut out up to 30 percent of that first pass. Think about the increased readability that enables.

- Double check grammar and spelling. But don't rely on grammar or spell check. The computer can't discriminate between to, two and too.

- Before pressing "send," consider the reader's work schedule. You may be working, but your audience may have a different schedule/time zone. Leverage Outlook functionality to delay delivery if appropriate.

Informational Email Examples

Original

Subject: Paper or Plastic?

The IRS has given taxpayers more opportunities to pay with plastic. This year individual taxpayers can use their credit cards to pay the balance due on their 2019 returns, pay a projected balance due when requesting an automatic extension of time to file a 2019 return and make estimated tax payments for 2019. In addition, they will no longer be required to file form 4868.

The pay-by-phone system will allow taxpayers to use American Express, Discover or MasterCard. This phone option, which started January 14, will be available for estimated tax payments on March 1, 2019.

Also, all individuals who file electronically – including those using TeleFile, the file by phone system – can choose to have the balance due debited directly from their bank accounts.

This sounds like a potential benefit, but how many readers are going to grasp the idea on the first – and only – read?

Suggested Revision:

Subject: Charge Your Tax Payments

The IRS now offers individual taxpayers the opportunity to charge their tax payments. The fee-based, pay-by-phone service accepts American Express, Discover, or MasterCard charges for:

- **The balance due on 2019 returns**

- **The projected balance due when requesting an automatic extension of time to file a 2019 return**

- **Estimated tax payments**

Further, you are not required to file form 4868.

File electronically (including by TeleFile, the file-by-phone system) and you can have the balance due debited directly from your bank accounts. For more information, contact me at _____.

Original

Subject: Time Stamping Bids

A few months ago we had training about stamping in bids when they are received at the front desk. Everything has been done correctly but I just wanted to remind you guys to tell anyone who happens to cover for you about the process of stamping in bids. See the excerpt below from the Purchasing Policy.

Receipt of Bids
Bids must be ...

When bids are received please time stamp them next to the company name on the address label. The buyer always cuts this out and puts it in the bid file to prove that the bid was submitted on time. Also, please initial by the time stamp. After you have stamped and initialed the bid, please put it on my desk and I will log it in.

It is important that everyone who fills in at the front desk knows these instructions so please forward this email to anyone who you think may help cover a shift in the future.

Please let me know if you have any questions.

Thank you!

Confusing right?

Possible Rewrite:

Subject: Reminder - Process of Stamping Bids

Employees who sit at the front desk handle the stampings of bids. When bids are received:

1) Time stamp the bid next to the company name on the address label.
2) Write your initials next to the stamp.
3) Place the bid or RFP on my desk.

This will ensure quality performance,

Original:

Re: New Department Supervisor

After weeks of deliberating, a decision has been made as to who would be Willie Leach's replacement. The management of the company has unanimously decided who the best person for the job is.

1 know many people have their own opinion on who should have been promoted and many more have opinions on whom not to give a chance too. Bottom line came down to who we felt had the best record of success with us as well as who wanted a long term association with the company.

There might have been some members of our staff that have been here longer, or that have shown more success but not in a consistent manner. Also when many of our top candidates were asked what their long-term goals were few stated a long run with our company.

Based on these criterions and the fact that we did not want to go though this search again in a year or so, we decided that Ashley Martinez is the best person for this job. Hopefully now that we have all our positions full we can get on with improving this company to the benefit of all of us.

Wouldn't you feel less warmed by your promotion if you were Ashley?

Possible Rewrite:

Subject: Ashley Martinez Named New Department Supervisor

Effective _____, Ashley Martinez will be the new Department Supervisor. Ms. Martinez:

- Joined the company on _____.

- Has ample experience in this role having served as _____.

Join me in the cafeteria at 3:00 to celebrate her new position

Original:

Subject: Email Server Maintenance

Tomorrow morning (Thursday May 12th) we'll be doing some maintenance on our email servers between 6:30 and 8:00am. Email services will not be available during that time. Service will be restored by 8:00am.

On Monday May 16th, a contractor will be on campus doing some additional work on our email servers. Each of our email servers (staff and client guests) will be down for about an hour and a half sometime around noon or later. When we have a better idea of the time we will send an email prior to the service interruption.

Possible Rewrite:

Subject: Email Server Maintenance Scheduled May 12 6:30 a.m. to 8:00 a.m. ET

Tomorrow morning (Thursday May 12th) we'll be doing some maintenance on our email servers between 6:30 and 8:00am. Email services will not be available during that time. Service will be restored by 8:00am.

Note: The second paragraph should be included in a second email only if and when it becomes necessary.

Original:

As managers, you are aware of the need to closely manage your capital expenditures. Several weeks ago, a list of capital procurement items was sent to each of you. You were instructed to proceed with purchasing those items for your particular department.

After careful review of the current year-end projections for various capital projects, it is necessary to halt certain capital expenditures.

The following list of items is on hold until further notice:
-
-
-
-

Please retain all procurement documents for these items and be prepared to proceed with purchase at a later date if we are able to release additional funds.

Possible Revision:

You each received a list of capital procurement items several weeks ago, and were instructed to proceed with purchasing those items for your particular department. Those purchases now need to be halted.

After completing a careful review of the current year-end projections for various capital projects, our CFO and COO have determined that, given our estimated income, we need to curtail certain capital expenditures until more business can be signed. There are several contracts pending so we hope to be able to release additional funds in the next quarter.

Stop any further activity on the purchase of the below listed items, but retain all procurement documents for future use.

Persuasive/Motivational Email Examples

Original:

NCP Leadership Team,

In preparation for our May 10 NCP Leadership planning meeting, I would like for you to be prepared to present your organization and the main issues you will be facing over the next 18 months. I would like for you to go into some depth on your analysis and keep in mind the budget initiatives we have in place for 2021.

For the second half of our meeting, I would like for you to address workforce-planning issues for your organization.

We are facing many challenges within our organization and our company. This meeting will be a springboard to address those issues and get us all on the same page and moving in the same direction.

Thank you for your effort and attention to detail and I look forward to a very productive meeting.

This was supposed to engender teamwork. Did you see how all the "I" statements negated that message? Look at the difference just taking those out makes.

Suggested Revision

It's time to prepare for the May 10 NCP Leadership planning meeting. At that time, you are expected to present your organization and the main issues you face over the next 18 months. Your analysis should be in some depth and considered in light of the budget initiatives in place for 2021.

During the second half of our meeting, we will discuss workforce-planning issues for your organization. Be prepared to expand that discussion.

We are facing many challenges within our company. This meeting is our opportunity for growth – a springboard to unifying our efforts so we move in the same direction.

Thank you for your effort and attention to detail. I look forward to a very productive meeting.

Original:

Subject: MIS Web Site

Mike,
About a week ago I started working on a first try at what I thought you would want the MIS site to look like. I was thinking you would want something clean and easy for the reader to browse. With that thought I started thinking that

following the OPS page layout to some degree would be the best option.

Emailing it to you does not seem to be possible so I put it up on Orange so that you can take a look. \\Orange\Fulfillment\myweb Once in the folder double click index.html

Don't worry about the links because most of that will change, be removed, or worked in differently I just needed to put something in those places for now. Most of the links will be worked into what will be the buttons on the left which will leave the right side open to awards, calendars, or what ever else we want.

What I talked about here is probably too much information but I wanted to at least show you the layout and see if I am going in the right direction.

Thanks

Possible Rewrite:

Mike,

The work on the MIS site has begun. We are going to follow the design of the OPS site to stay consistent. When you have time, take a look at it on the server under \\Orange\Fulfillment\myweb

Ignore the content. Just look at the design and let me know if you are ok with it.

I'll continue working on this project once I hear from you.

Original:

To: All Sales Reps
Subject: Power Mate Gear Reducers

Starting with June shipments, all Power Mate gear reducers will have new and improved shaft seals. We have made the popular double lip seal standard across the line. This superior sealing system stands up to tough applications two and a half times better than the previous single lip seal systems.

We are offering this added feature at no additional cost. Please use the attached data sheet to explain the features and benefits of this new seal to your customers. We will be happy to help you work through any non-standard applications.

Thank you for your support. Please call me if you have any questions.

Who's getting the email? Sales people.

What do sales people care about? Making money.

So this email would be more motivational if it were to read:

Possible Rewrite:

To: All Sales Reps
Subject: Power Mate Gear Reducers

Starting with June shipments, all Power Mate gear reducers will have new and improved shaft seals. These popular double lip seals:

- Will be standard across the line.

- Stand up to tough applications two and a half times better than the previous single lip seal systems.

- Be available at no additional cost.

Review the attached data sheets and let's talk about how you can close more sales.

NEXT STEPS

Okay, take a breath. This is a lot to take in, but you did it. Your next steps?

- Choose one or two behavioral changes that make sense to you, changes that you think will improve your writing. Work with those for three weeks.

- Monitor your responses after three weeks. See if your level of satisfactory replies increases.

- Come back for more new approaches.

- Congratulate yourself for making the decision to improve.

> **Be an amateur. Not everything you do has to be good, especially at first.**
>
> *— Ann Handley, Chief Content Officer, Marketing Profs*

My prediction? Any change you make will increase your ability to better inform, persuade and/or motivate your reader in the direction you want – and with less effort than you have expended in the past. As important, the communications skills you gain will spell more opportunities in your future!

In fact, let me know what changes you see or questions that arise as you move forward.

Wishing you success,
Claudia Coplon Clements

Claudiac@execspeakwrite.com
www.executivespeakwrite.com

REFERENCE MATERIALS

Resources

The Elements of Style
William Strunk, Jr., and E.B. White

Send
David Shipley and Will Schwalbe

Eats, Shoots & Leaves: The Zero Tolerance Approach to Punctuation
Lynne Truss

Writing Effective Letters, Memos, & Email
Arthur H. Bell, Ph.D.

Business Letters That Get Results!
J. Hamilton Jones

http://public.wsu.edu/~brians/errors/errors.html

https://www.grammarly.com/

Purdue University's Online Writing Lab:
http://owl.english.purdue.edu/owl/section/1/1/

Your Turn

Revise these 21 words down to 8 or 9:

It was a 20-minute period of time after the accident had occurred when the emergency vehicles arrived to lend assistance.

Possible Revision:

Emergency vehicles arrived to lend assistance 20 minutes after the accident.

- Adding to "lend assistance" is important, as the reader needs to know what the vehicles did.

- "After the accident" matters, as the reader needs to know what happened.

Revise the following 21 words down to 12:

It was decided that the club would organize a committee for the purpose of conducting a search for a new leader.

Possible Revision:

The club will organize a committee to search for a new leader.

- Were you to write, "the club organized," you will generate responses from those angry they were not included on the committee.

- Indicating that "the club" will handle the organizing tells the reader who will be handling the process.

Identifying Passive Voice

On MAC

1. Launch Word.
2. Go to the top menu bar, Word > Preferences.
3. Select the "Spelling and Grammar" icon.
4. Put a selection mark for "Check grammar as you type."
5. Set "Writing Style" drop list to "Formal".

In MS Word

1. Open the document to edit in Word.
2. Click "File," and then click "Options" to launch the Word Options dialog box.
3. Click "Proofing" in the Word Options dialog box.
4. Click the "Settings" button in the When Correcting Spelling and Grammar in Word Section. The Proofing Settings dialog box opens.
5. Scroll down to Styles and click the "Passive Sentences" option. Select other options in the dialog box, as desired. Click "OK" to close the box.
6. Click the "Mark Grammar Errors As You Type" check box in the Proofing dialog box. Click "OK" to save the settings and close the Proofing dialog box.
7. Click the "Review" tab, and then click "Spelling & Grammar" to manually check the document.

CLAUDIA COPLON CLEMENTS BIO

For 20+ years, Claudia Coplon Clements has trained professionals to generate concise, relationship-building written communications. Her goal? To help employees, managers and executives overcome life-long phobias and poor writing habits. Claudia's non-threatening, humorous corporate training programs enable participants to improve business writing skills, inspire confidence and create more effective written communications.

Her expertise is founded in having developed, organized, coordinated and prepared written materials, strategic communications and public relations programs for companies in public and private sectors. These company industries include, but are not limited to, engineering, high tech, food and food packaging, academia, transportation and logistics, health care, finance, consumer, association, legal, and business-to-business.

Consequently, Claudia brings to her training and coaching real life experience coupled with tried and true public relations approaches and a drive to conciseness. Her business writing training blends writing basics and direction within the jargons specific to each client's industry.

From correctional professionals working in New Mexico, Tennessee and Alaska prisons to CEOs in boardrooms across the U.S. and staff at educational institutions such as Emory University, University of Georgia, Spelman College and North Carolina State, Claudia conveys skills that declutter the written word and attract reader attention. As a result, clients gain the skills and philosophy necessary to position their written materials for impact, make their point and get results.

Claudiac@execspeakwrite.com
www.executivespeakwrite.com

Made in the USA
Monee, IL
04 November 2021